Dangerous Stunts

Jonny Zucker

FULL FLIGHT

Titles in Full Flight 3

Badger Publishing Limited
26 Wedgwood Way, Pin Green Industrial Estate, Stevenage,
Hertfordshire SG1 4QF
Telephone: 01438 356907. Fax: 01438 747015.
www.badger-publishing.co.uk
enquiries@badger-publishing.co.uk

Dangerous Stunts   ISBN 1 84424 249 8

Text © Jonny Zucker 2004
Series editing © Jonny Zucker 2004
Complete work © Badger Publishing Limited 2004

Series Editor: Jonny Zucker
Editor: Paul Martin
Cover photo: The Rookie
Photos: © The Kobal Collection
7/Warner, 11/Fox, P. Lo
14/Golden Harvest, 31/
© Rex Features; pp. 16;
© Topham Picturepoint

Dangerous Stunts

Jonny Zucker

Contents

Badger Publishing

1. What is a Stunt?

There are two main types of stunt:

- Stunts in films (pages 5-21).

- Stunts performed by magicians and escape artists (pages 22-31).

2. So you want to be in the Movies?

Have you ever watched a film, seen someone jumping out of a window or crashing a helicopter, and thought I'd like to do that? The job of a stunt artist is to perform dangerous acts to add excitement to a film. For anyone wanting to become a stunt artist, the training is long and very hard.

For a start you have to be very fit, willing to learn and not be scared of getting hurt.

You might need to:

- Perform 'high jumps' off buildings or from the top of high ladders.
- Have mock fights that look real but don't hurt anyone.
- Become very good at driving cars at top speed without crashing.
- Learn how to steer a boat or fly a plane.

Even if you become a trained stunt artist, you may still not get any parts in films. There are lots of stunt artists trying to make it into movies. If you do get film parts, you could find yourself at a cinema watching yourself diving off a cliff, having a sword fight or being blown up.

3. Body Doubles

Body doubles are people who take the place of actors in stunt scenes. Many actors are not willing or able to perform their own stunts. They're not fit enough, they haven't had the right training or they simply don't want to put themselves in any kind of danger.

For a stunt scene, the body double is dressed in the same clothes as the actor. They may have to wear a wig or body padding. These scenes are filmed so that no one can tell it's a body double, not the actor, flying off that mountain or leaping into a waterfall.

Some stunt scenes are filmed from a distance or from a different angle, so that you can't properly see the body double's face. If you look very carefully, in some films it is possible to spot body doubles.

Vic Armstrong was the stunt artist who stood in for Harrison Ford in the Indiana Jones films. When asked what was the hardest stunt he had to perform in these movies, he joked:

> **Keeping the hat on in**
> ***Raiders of the Lost Ark!***

4. Stunt Co-ordinators

Every film with stunts has a stunt co-ordinator. The job of a stunt co-ordinator is to make a stunt scene as real and as safe as possible.

Sometimes the stunt will only need one or two people, but at other times a whole team of stunt artists will be needed. The stunt co-ordinator makes a plan of everything that will happen in a stunt scene.

The stunt co-ordinator then talks everyone through the scene. The stunt artists will learn the exact positions they need to be in and the moves they'll have to make.

It is important that everyone understands their role, because even the smallest mistake could make the stunt more dangerous than it needs to be. When the stunt co-ordinator feels his team are ready, the scene can be filmed. Even when the cameras are rolling, there might have to be several 'takes' to get the scene right.

Shooting stunt scenes in Steve Oedekerk's *Kung Pow: Enter the Fist.*

5. Actors who do it themselves

Some actors choose to perform most or all of their stunts themselves and don't use body doubles. Film directors are not always happy about this. They worry that the actor may get hurt or isn't properly trained. Some stunt co-ordinators are also unhappy about actors doing stunts. They think that work is being taken away from trained stunt artists.

Here are some actors who have done some stunts themselves:

- Pierce Brosnan in his Bond films.
- Angelina Jolie in the Tomb Raider films.
- Daniel Radcliffe, who played the hero in the first Harry Potter films.

Daniel Radcliffe says:

I do as many of my own stunts as possible, but there are some things I can't do.

6. Martial Arts Film Stunts

These films contain kung fu, karate and other martial arts. Many of the actors are trained in martial arts and don't need stunt artists to replace them in fight scenes. The most famous martial arts movie star of all time is Jackie Chan, who has made many films and has millions of fans all over the world.

Martial arts stunts have not just been used in films and TV shows. Many TV adverts have fight scenes and several advertising posters have used pictures of martial arts fighting.

7. Stunt Driving

The car chase is a must in many action films. Writers and directors are always trying out new types of chase, with faster cars and more dangerous scenes. Some stunt training courses expect stunt drivers to drive at very fast speeds down narrow country lanes without damaging the car or getting hurt.

To become a stunt driver takes thousands of hours of training. Stunt drivers must learn to:

1) Skid and turn at high speeds without crashing their car.
2) Spin off bridges.
3) Smash into other vehicles.
4) Turn cars upside down.

8. The Name's Bond

James Bond films are well known for their stunts. There are always a large number of stunt men and women on the set of a Bond film. In every film, Bond will be involved in some incredible fights and do some amazing stunts as he fights evil.

The most famous stunt in a Bond film took place at the start of *Goldeneye*. Stunt artist Wayne Michaels did a bungee jump off a gigantic dam. It was a highly dangerous act and he knew if it went wrong he was sure to get very badly hurt. He looked at the waiting ambulances just before he jumped and shouted:

OK, stretchers ready.

Wayne Michaels (right) recieves an award for the *Goldeneye* stunt.

9. Stunts and Computers

Some films use a mix of real stunts and special effects to create film scenes. One of the best-known films to mix the two is *The Matrix*. In one of the opening scenes, a woman incredibly appears to run round walls as she tries to escape an attacker.

In *The Lord of the Rings* you can see some of the most fantastic scenes in the history of cinema. Real stunt artists were used to make some of the fight scenes, but computers added thousands of extra warriors to battle scenes. This was done so well that anyone watching finds it hard to believe that the scene is not totally 'real'.

10. Houdini and the art of Escaping

Houdini was the most famous escape artist of all time. He started off by doing magic tricks, but soon saw that people loved shows with plenty of danger. So he started performing escape stunts. At first, he was locked up in handcuffs and was able to break free.

It wasn't long before he was locked up inside a cage filled with water and inside a locked prison cell. He was able to escape from both of these. Houdini's most famous escape stunt saw him being chained up and put into a locked wooden crate. This crate was then thrown into a river.

When he didn't appear straight away, many people thought Houdini had died, but he was seen swimming in the water and waving to the crowd. For this stunt Houdini used two secret tricks. First of all, he was carrying a lock pick in a hidden pocket. Secondly, the wooden crate had a secret panel at one end that was easy to kick off and so escape.

11. The Death Dive

American Robert Gallup did one of the most dangerous stunts of all time in 1996. If he didn't get everything right, there was no way that Gallup was going to stay alive. For this stunt:

- He was tied up in heavy metal chains and locked inside a small metal cage.

- This cage was then put into a plane that flew several thousand metres into the sky.

- The cage was then pushed out of the plane with Gallup inside.

He knew he had only 50 seconds to escape before the cage crashed onto the land below and killed him.

Incredibly, he managed to get out of the chains, open the cage door and grab the parachute waiting for him on the outside of the cage.

He got out with only a few seconds to spare.

12. Driven over by a Lorry

Penn and Teller are American performers who enjoy breaking the first rule of magic; they often tell TV viewers how their tricks are done. Many other magicians are angry with them for breaking this rule, but they carry on doing it.

One of their best stunts involved Teller lying on the ground and being 'run over' by an enormous lorry. The wheels of the lorry seemed to drive over Teller's head, yet he wasn't hurt in any way. How on earth was this possible? Penn told everyone how this stunt was done.

- The lorry they used had one side weighed down with a very heavy load.

- The other side had no weight on it at all and was raised off the ground by the weight on the other side.
- The tyres on this 'light' side were made of foam and these gently rolled over Teller's head as the lorry moved forward.

By using this simple idea, they made the whole thing look so real.

13. Roller Coaster Stunt

For this stunt, American magician and escape artist Lance Burton, was tied to the tracks of a very fast roller coaster. Armed only with some lock picks he had less than a minute to free himself from the track and escape being killed.

As the clock ticked away, the roller coaster sped round the track and anyone watching felt sure that Burton had taken on a stunt too far. As the roller coaster got within a few metres of Burton, he managed to leap up and dive off the track. As with all stunt scenes on TV, Burton could have 'faked' the stunt, by using 'trick photography', but knowing his love of danger, it probably was real.

14. The Ice Man

American David Blaine has become one of
the greatest stunt artists in the world.
Harry Houdini is his great hero and Blaine
wants to be as well liked as Houdini was in
his lifetime. Blaine is a very fine magician,
but he also takes part in 'endurance tests'.
He says that he likes putting his mind and
body under great pressure to see how well
he can handle it.

Blaine suspended above London for 44 days without food, Sept 2003.

Blaine has been 'buried alive' in a coffin for one week, has stood on top of the London Eye and has jumped from a high pole with only cardboard boxes to break his fall. For his most famous act, he was placed inside a giant block of ice for 63 hours. Some doctors had stated that Blaine could become very ill if he went ahead with this stunt and could even die.

Blaine didn't listen to them and went ahead with the stunt. There was a camera crew there the whole time, so it is almost impossible that Blaine cheated. After coming out of the ice, he was rushed to hospital for check ups and claimed that it took him a month to get over his 63 hours in the ice.

15. Danger!

All of the people in this book have put themselves in different kinds of danger. And for a stunt to go right, there are many things that need to go to plan. Stunt artists need to listen to their stunt co-ordinators, practise until they are confident and make sure their timing is perfect.

Although stunts are made as safe as possible, stunt artists and escape artists can get badly hurt. There are always things that can go wrong. They may lose their footing, jump too early or lose control of a speeding car. Sometimes equipment can fail even if it's been checked and checked again.

Stunt artists have been hurt many times, from getting slightly burnt to breaking an arm. In the worst cases, some stunt artists have died.

So there's a lot to think about if you're really serious about becoming a stunt artist or an escape artist and there are years of training. If you do make it, who knows, the sky may be the limit!

Index